MY MOUNTAIN STAR

Author Albert Becerra

Illustrations by Mozelle Espino

REGAN ST. PUBLISHING
EST. 2023
ARLINGTON, TX

©Albert Becerra-Regan St. Publishing- Mozelle Espino

Copyright © 2023 Albert Becerra Illustrations copyright © 2023 Mozelle Espino. All rights reserved. No part of this book may be reproduced or transmitted in any form or by any means, electronic or mechanical, including photocopying, recording, or by any information storage and retrieval system, without written permission from the author. For information address Albert Becerra: becerracreativegroup@gmail.com

Printed in the U.S.A
9798218169077

Cover design by Mozelle Espino
Edited by Deborah Falls

This book is dedicated to everyone in my beautiful hometown of El Paso, TX. I hope you see yourself represented in my love for our city and its iconic star. Most importantly, my grandmother Bertha Carrillo. She always pushed me to do more in education. To my mother and wife, thank you for your constant support throughout this process!
To all my former teachers and educators that have helped me get this book together. To my family and friends, thank you for inspiring the characters in this story.
Lastly, to my children who inspired me to write this book in an effort to have more of themselves represented. I love you so much my darling Aria & Benjamin!

"Dios los bendiga, y bendiga a tus hijos!"
Bertha Carrillo

This is a story about a young El Pasoan trying to find out what the iconic star on the Franklin Mountains means. Through his journey, he realizes how important such a landmark can be. I hope that it inspires you to think about the star and what it means to you. For those of us outside of the city, who have started our lives away from the border town, I hope that it gives you that warm fuzzy feeling I get whenever I see that star glowing in the distance! I hope you enjoy it!
-Albert

"Okay Paco, it's time to go mimis. Turn off the light, rezale a la virgencita and go to sleep! Ya es tarde!" said Paco's mom Letty.

"Okay, Mom! Oye ma', what's the star on the mountain mean?" asks Paco

"Well... to me I'm reminded of when your Uncle Mark and the troops from Ft. Bliss came home from the war. It was a way to help us have faith that they were coming home safe."

"Wow!" says Paco surprised

Letty says, "Bueno ya mijo... a dormir!"

Paco responds, "Yes ma'am!"

The next morning at the kitchen table Paco says to his Grandpa Benny, "Oye Apa, que significa la estrella en la montaña?" (Grandpa, what does the star on the mountain mean?) Grandpa Benny responds, "Pues mijo...es una estrella que es para todos. Es el símbolo de la ciudad." ("Well mijo, it's a star that's for everyone. It's a symbol of the city.")

While Grandma Bertha washes dishes she tells Paco, "Para mi mijo, me ayuda ubicarme en dónde estoy en la ciudad. Cuando voy hacia la estrella se que voy para el centro." ("For me Mijo, it helps me find where I am in the city. When I'm going towards the star I'm going Downtown.")

"Ahh okay." Paco says in a pensive mood

After breakfast, Paco tells his mom he's going bike riding with Joel. On his way to Joel's house, he stops by the tire shop. Paco yells out, "Don Luis, ¿Me llena la llanta?" ("Mr. Luis, can you fill my tire?")

As he fills the tire with air Paco asks, "Don Luis, what does the star mean to you?" Don Luis responds, "Well Paquito... to me it means freedom. When my family came over from Juarez it was one the first things I saw." Paco smiles and says, "Oh, so it must mean a lot, huh?" "Sure does!" smiled Don Luis. Paco yells out "Muchas Gracias!" as he rides away

Paco rides off and meets Joel. Paco yells out, "Hey Güero!!" Joel yells out, "Hey Paco!!" Paco asks, "Hey Güero, You know the star on the mountain? What does the star mean to you?" Joel thinks for a moment and responds, "Well, my mom says that the star was lit for Christmas like an ornament, so I guess to me it reminds me of Christmas and the buñuelos your apa makes" Paco says, "Órale! Race you to Loretto!" Güero responds, "Loser buys licuados (fruit shake) at Jr's!" "You're on!" yells Paco.

That evening Paco and his family are at his cousin Valerie's quinceañera. Paco enjoying the music asks a mariachi, "Señor what does the star mean to you?" The mariachi thinks a bit and responds, "Bueno mijo, to me it means pride!" Paco responds puzzled, "Pride?"
"Si! When I see that star lit up, it's a reminder of how much pride I have to be from El Chucho!" replies the mariachi. Paco responds, "Ohhh…Gracias Señor!"

Later that night, when it's time for bed, Letty tells Paco, "Bueno mijo, mimis time, you had a busy day!"

"Si, mami! Guess what I found out??" Paco says.

"What?" his mom responds curiously.

Paco says proudly, "The star means something different to everyone!"

"Oh really, and what does it mean to you?" Letty asks.

Paco is now an adult and has a wife and a little girl. As they're walking in the park, his daughter Aria asks, "Daddy, do you see the star on that mountain?" Paco responds, "Si mija?"

"What does it mean?" she asks.

"Well… it means many things to many people."

Aria looks confused and asks, "What does it mean to you?"

Paco responds, "To me?… To me, it means home!"

Albert Becerra
Author

Albert Becerra was born and raised in Central El Paso. Attending Hillside Elementary, Ross MS, and Burges HS. He holds a B.S. in Liberal Studies from Arizona State University and an M.Ed in Educational Leadership from the University of North Texas. He currently resides in Arlington, TX with his wife Beatriz and their children Aria and Benjamin. He previously taught mariachi music and is now a high school assistant principal. He wrote this story during the start of the pandemic. He missed his hometown and his beloved star on the mountain.

Mozelle Espino
Illustrator

Mozelle is a 22-year-old artist born and raised at El Paso, TX. With a passion for art, she has worked hard on her hobby at a young age in pursuit of becoming a full-time career. This is her first time working on the illustrations for a book, which has been a great experience for her. She looks forward to drawing more and improving her skills to be a better artist every day.

History about the star

According to the El Paso Times, the Star on the Mountain was first lighted in 1940 by the El Paso Electric Company and became a Christmas tradition. It's been used as a symbol of hope throughout hostage situations and wars. Many improvements have come since including a larger star and an improved lighting system. It has been under the care of the Greater El Paso Chamber of Commerce and El Paso Electric Co. in a joint project. It continues to be a unique symbol in the borderland for many generations of El Pasoans and those visiting the "Sun City".

This page intentionally left blank.

CPSIA information can be obtained
at www.ICGtesting.com
Printed in the USA
BVHW060947200423
662718BV00003B/59